About Kiss My Ass

Outstanding Swear Word To Color For Stress Releasing

Ja Millie Hawthorn

Happy Coloring!

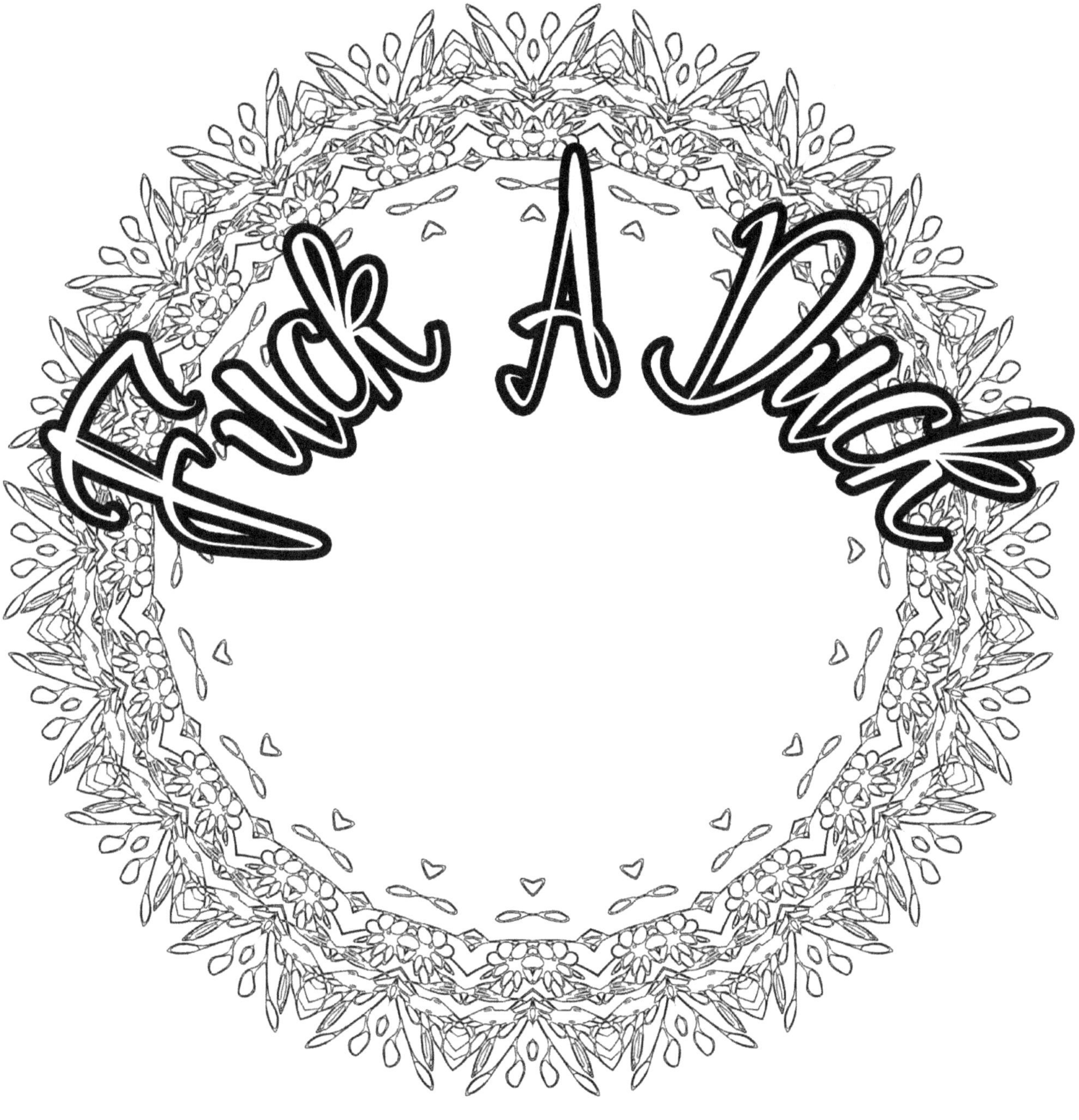
Fuck A Duck

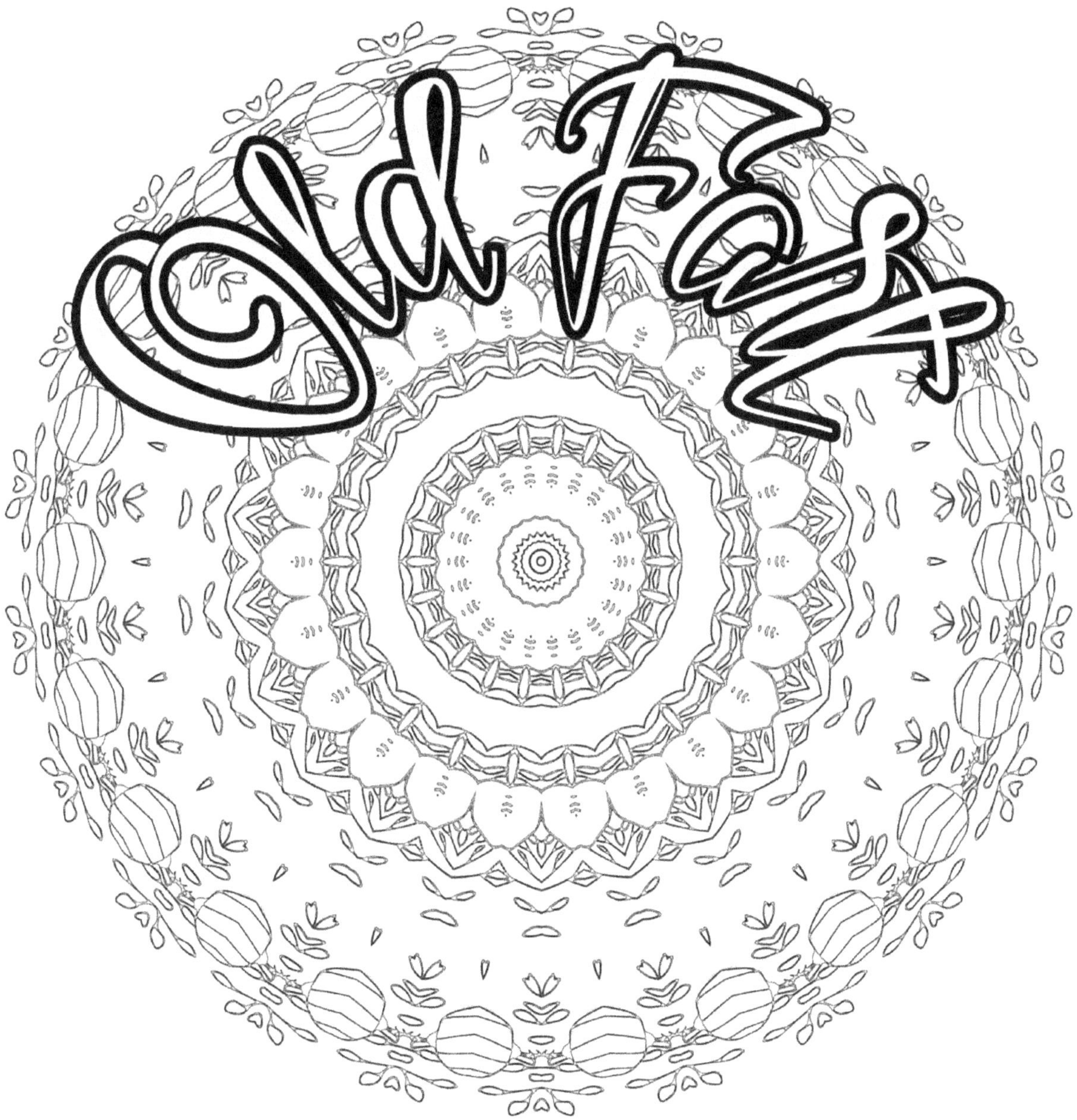
Old Fart

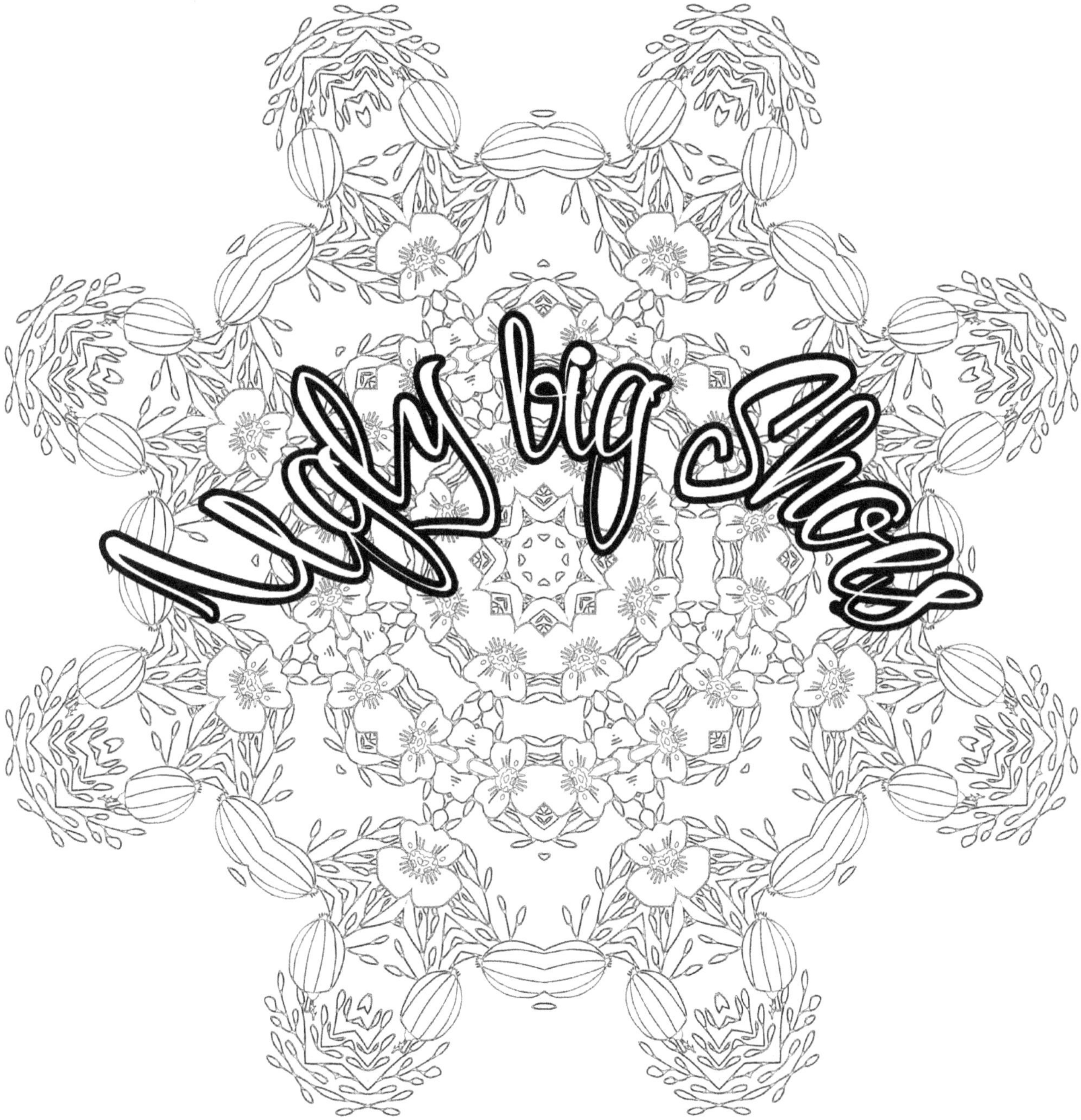
Ugly big Shoes

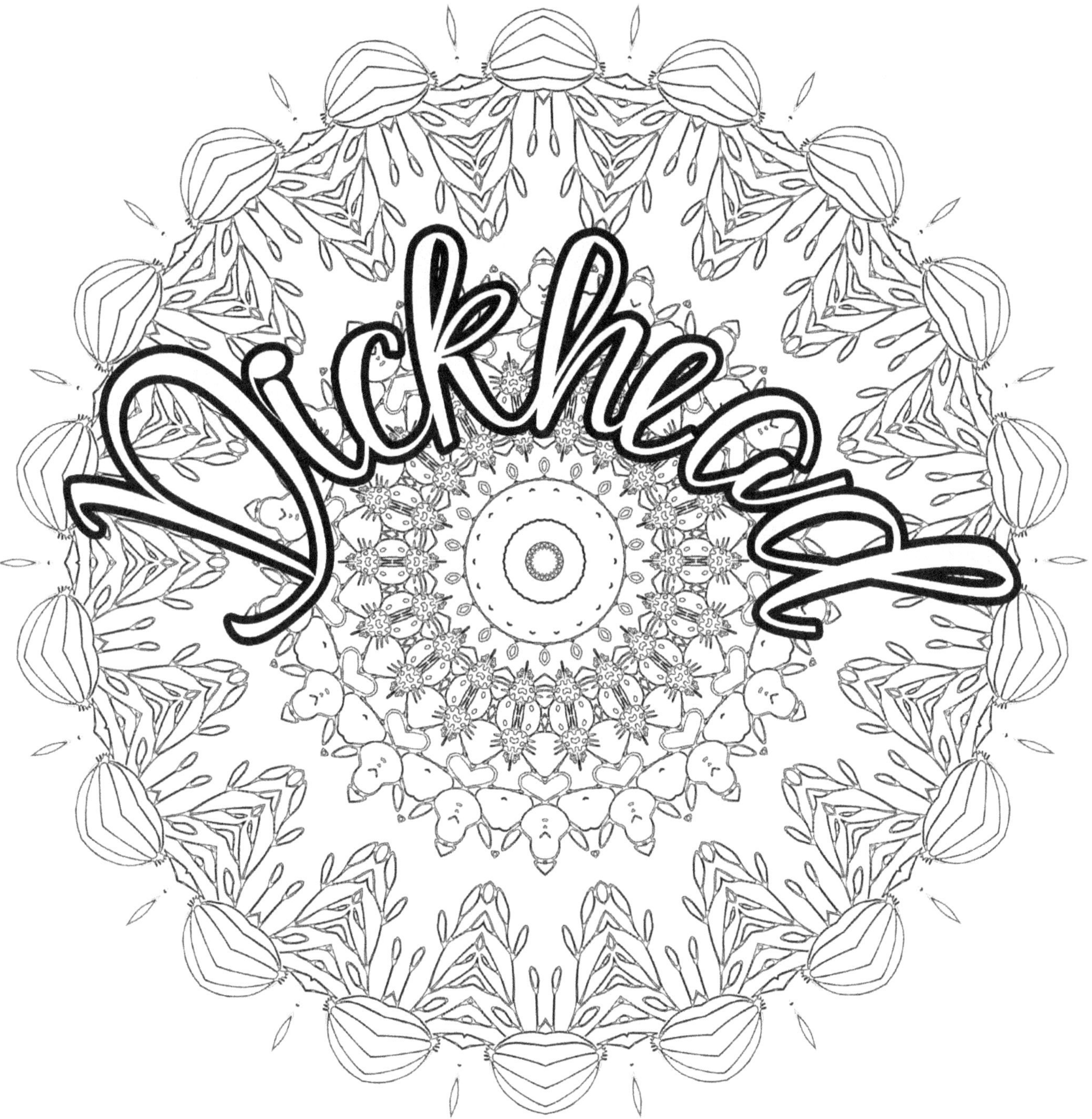
Dickhead

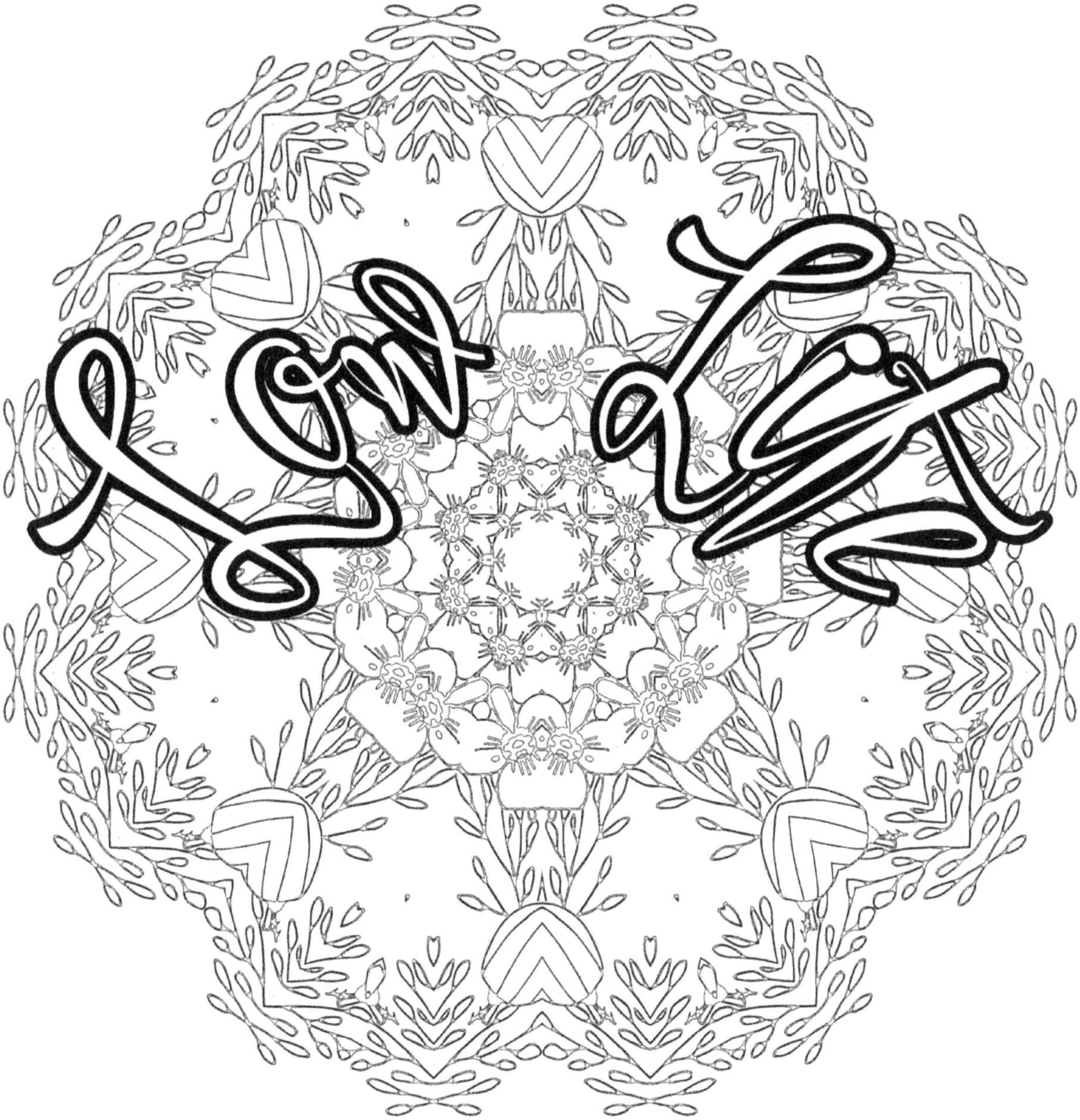
Love Life

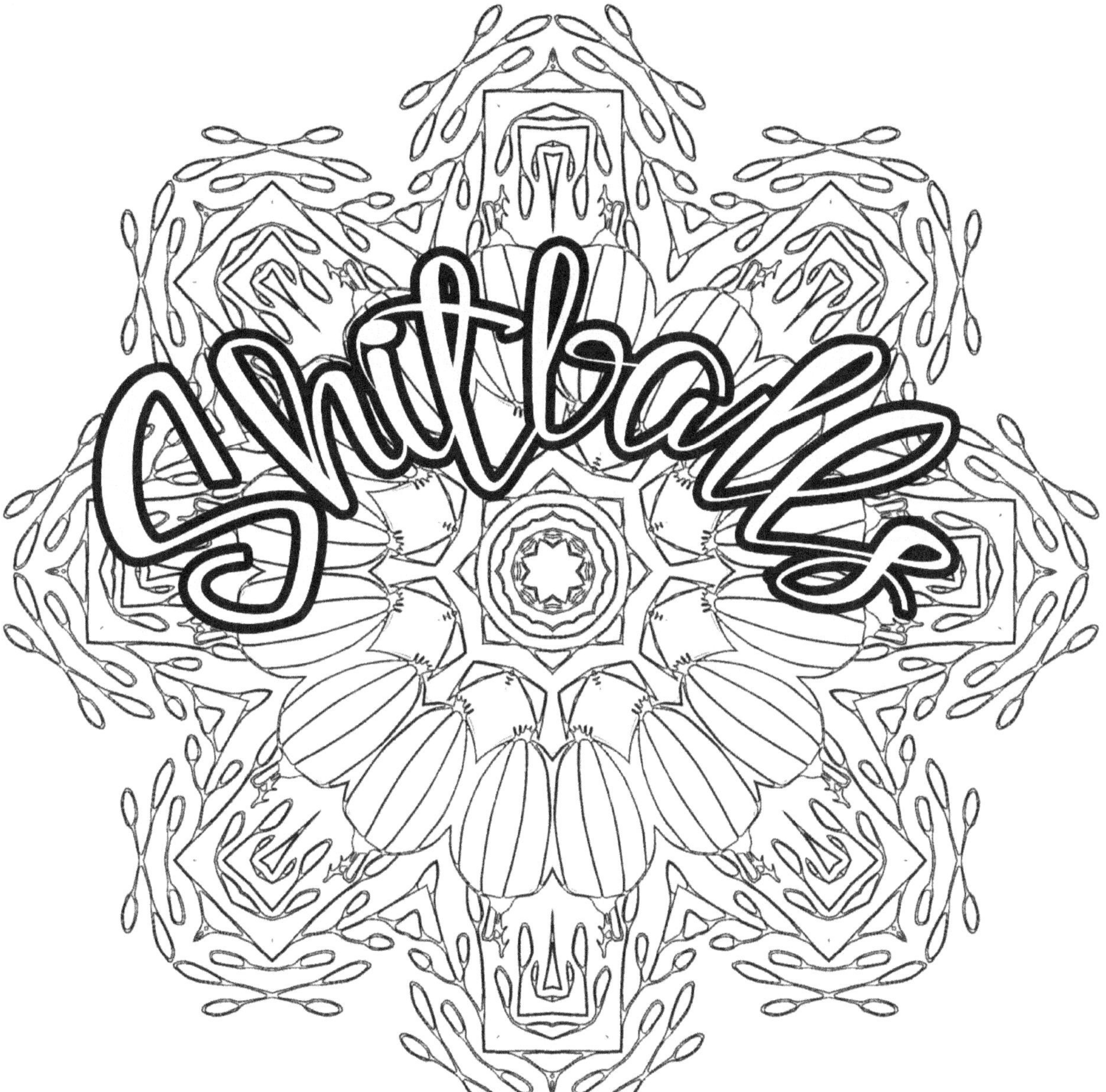
Shitballs

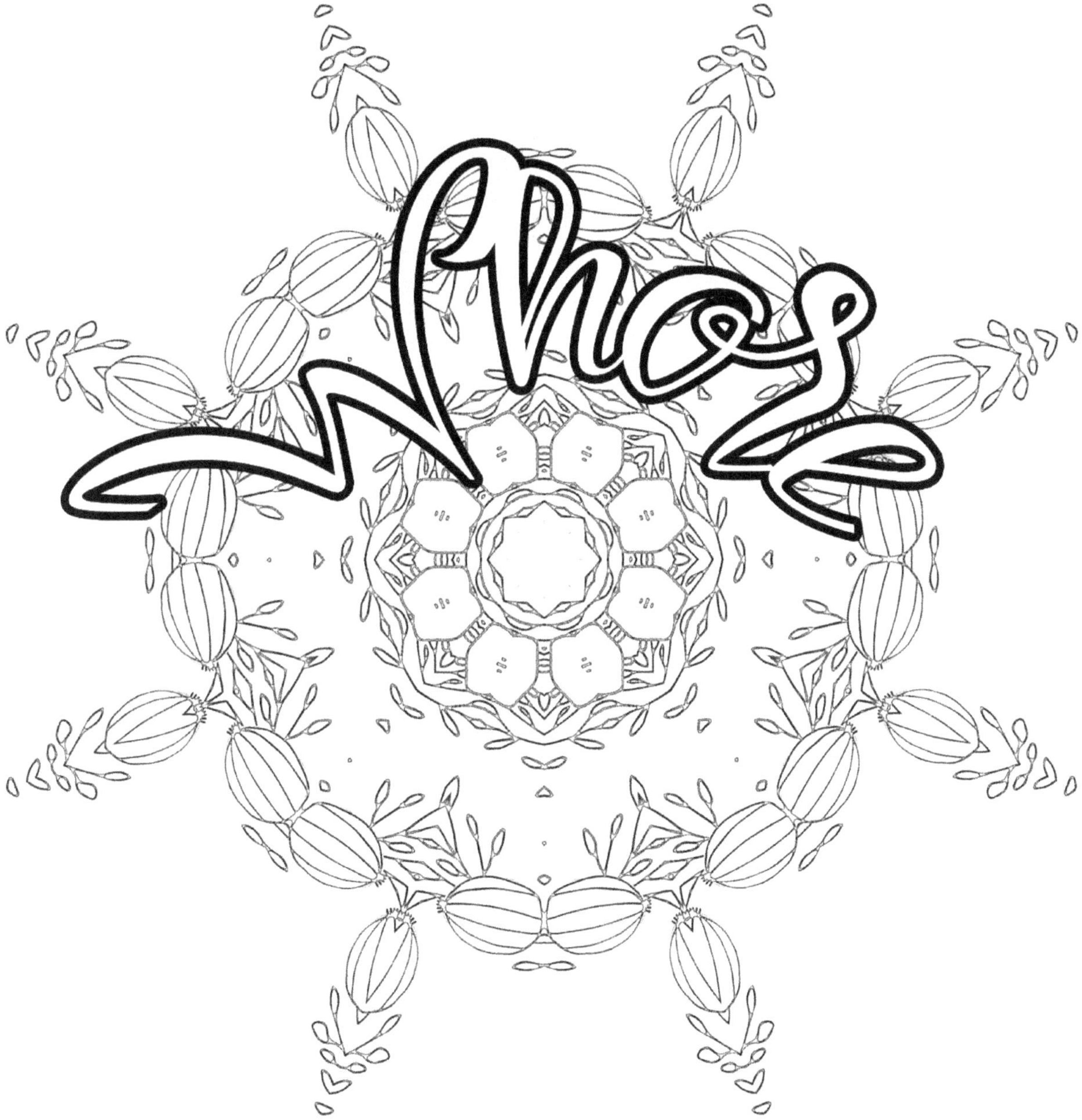

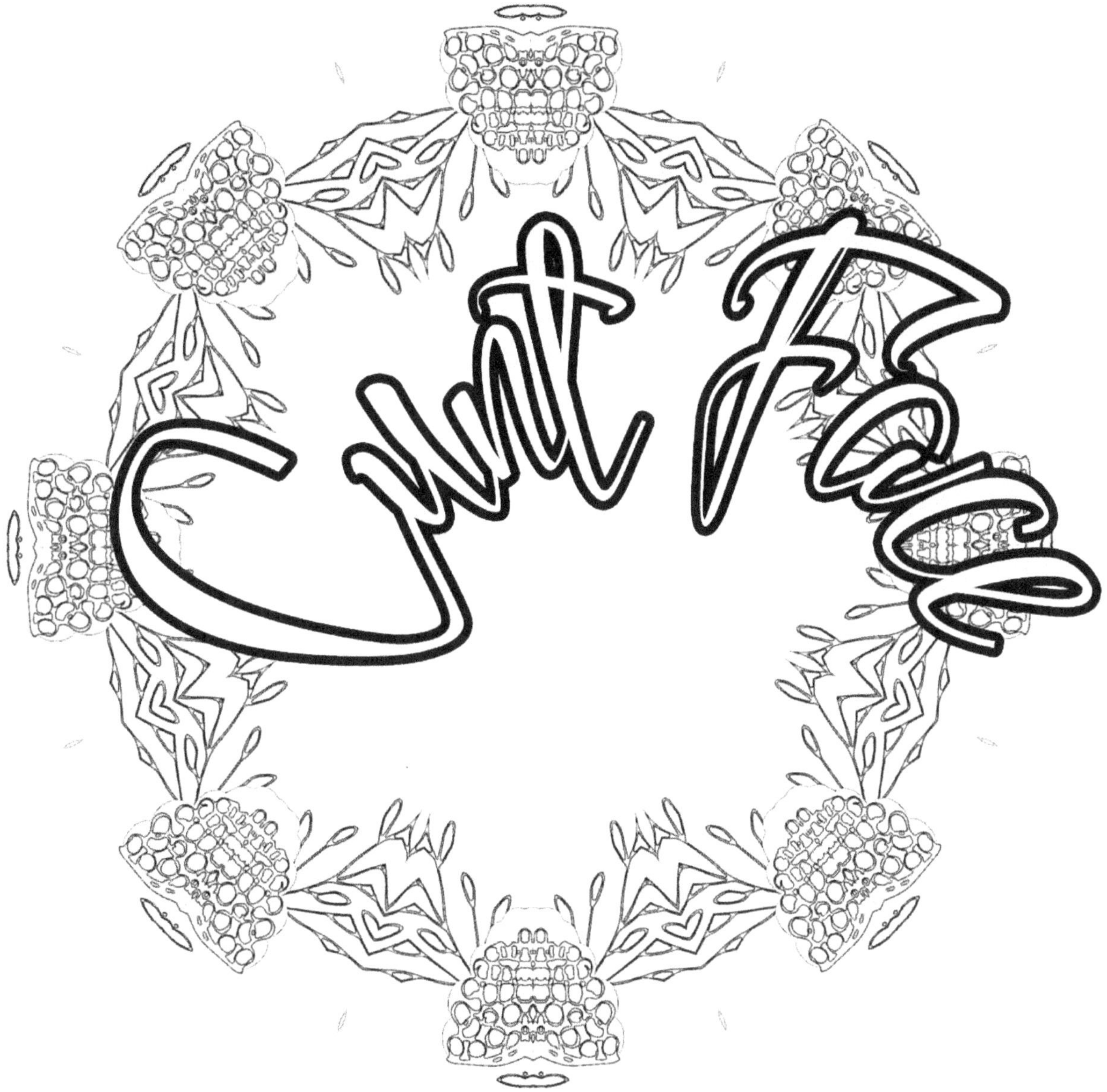
Cunt Face

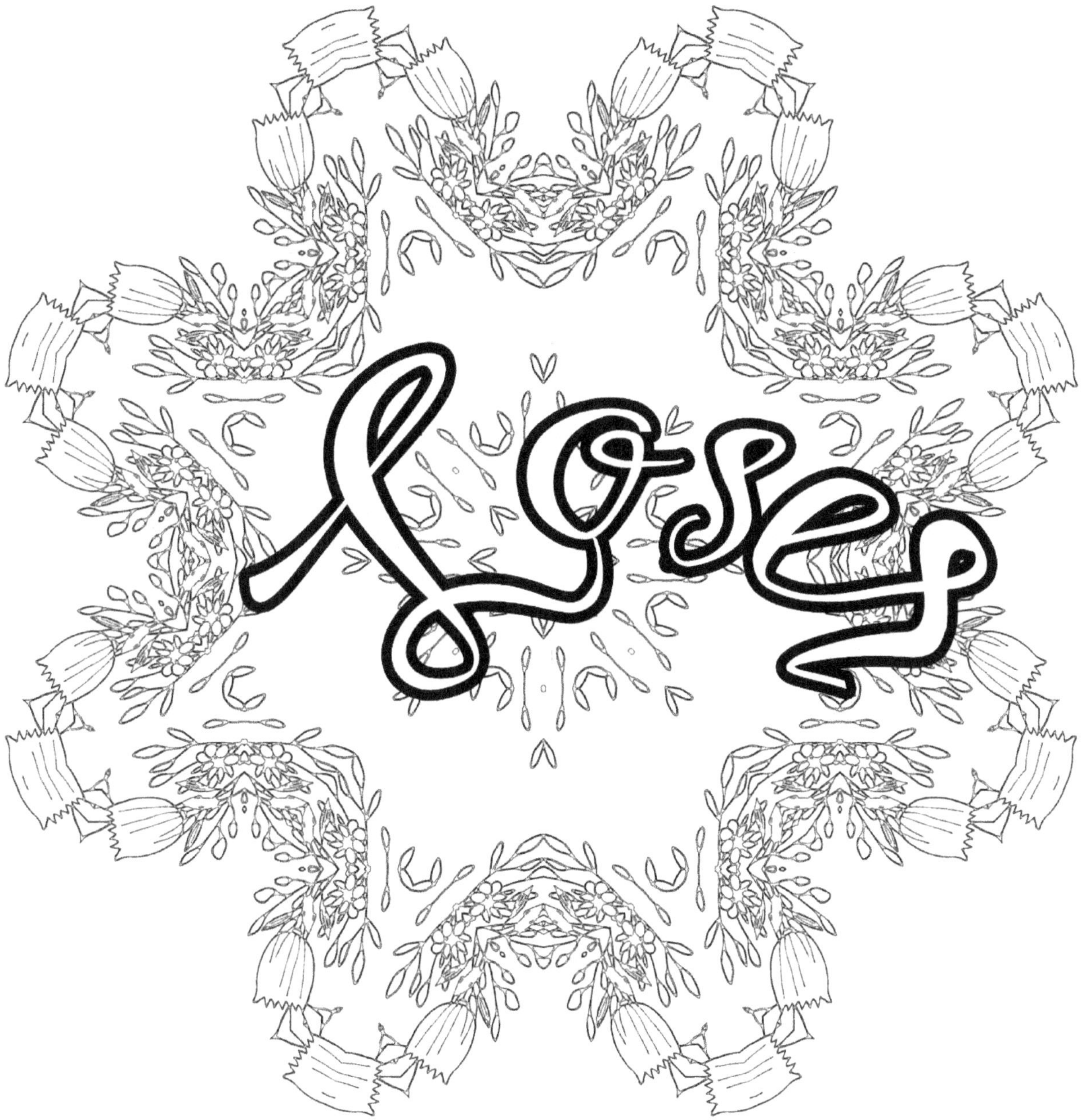
Loser

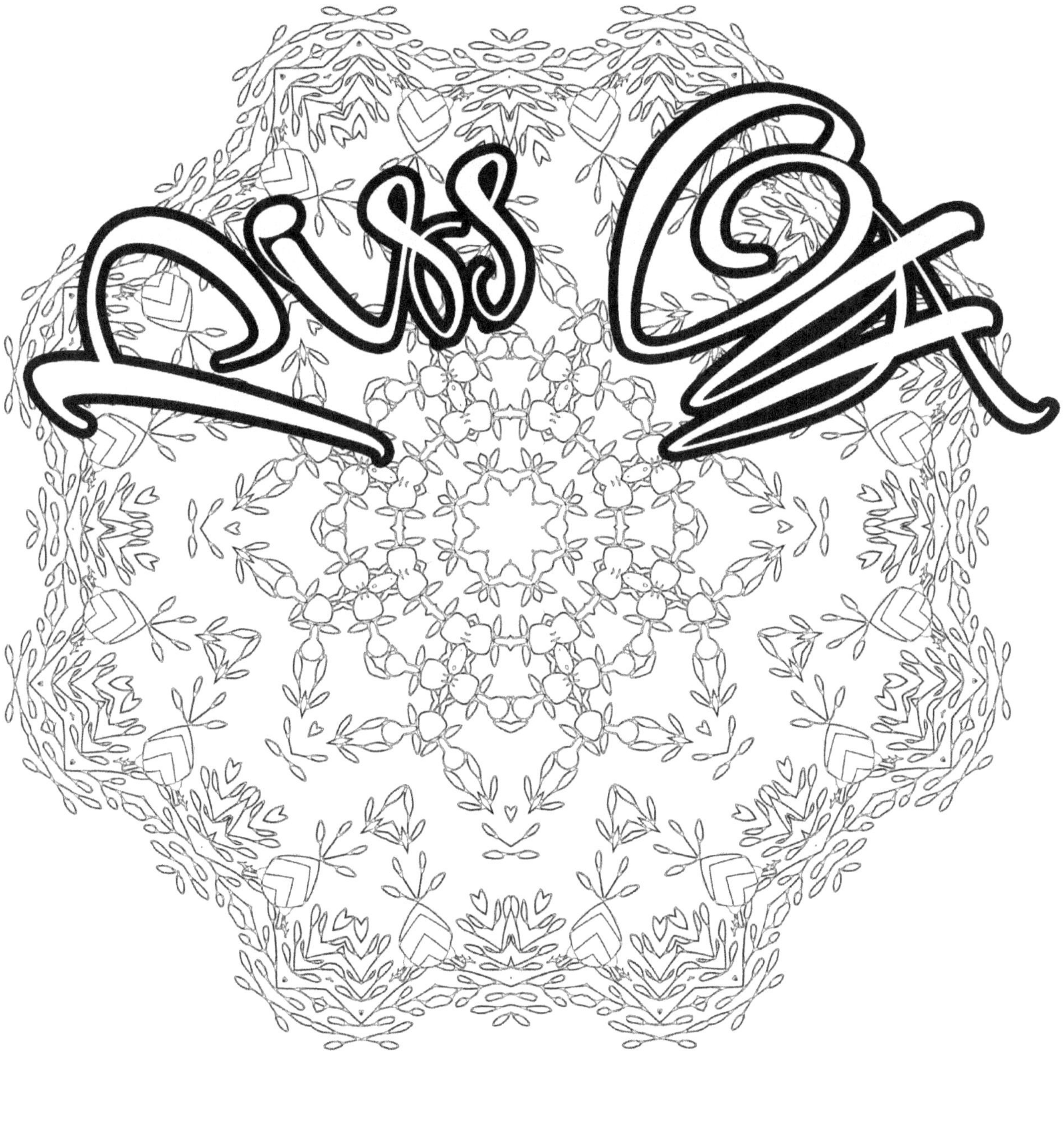
Piss Off

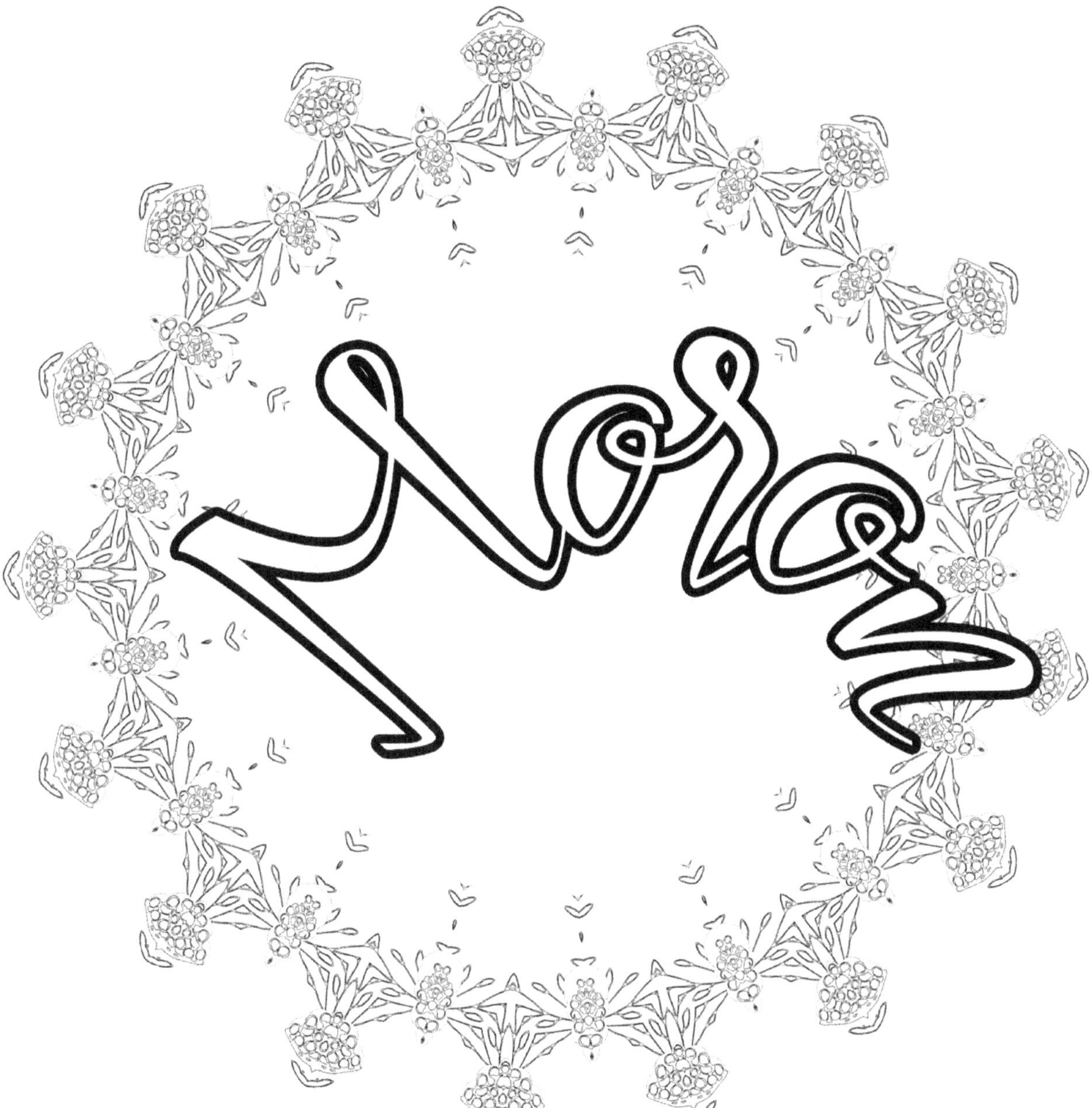
Noran

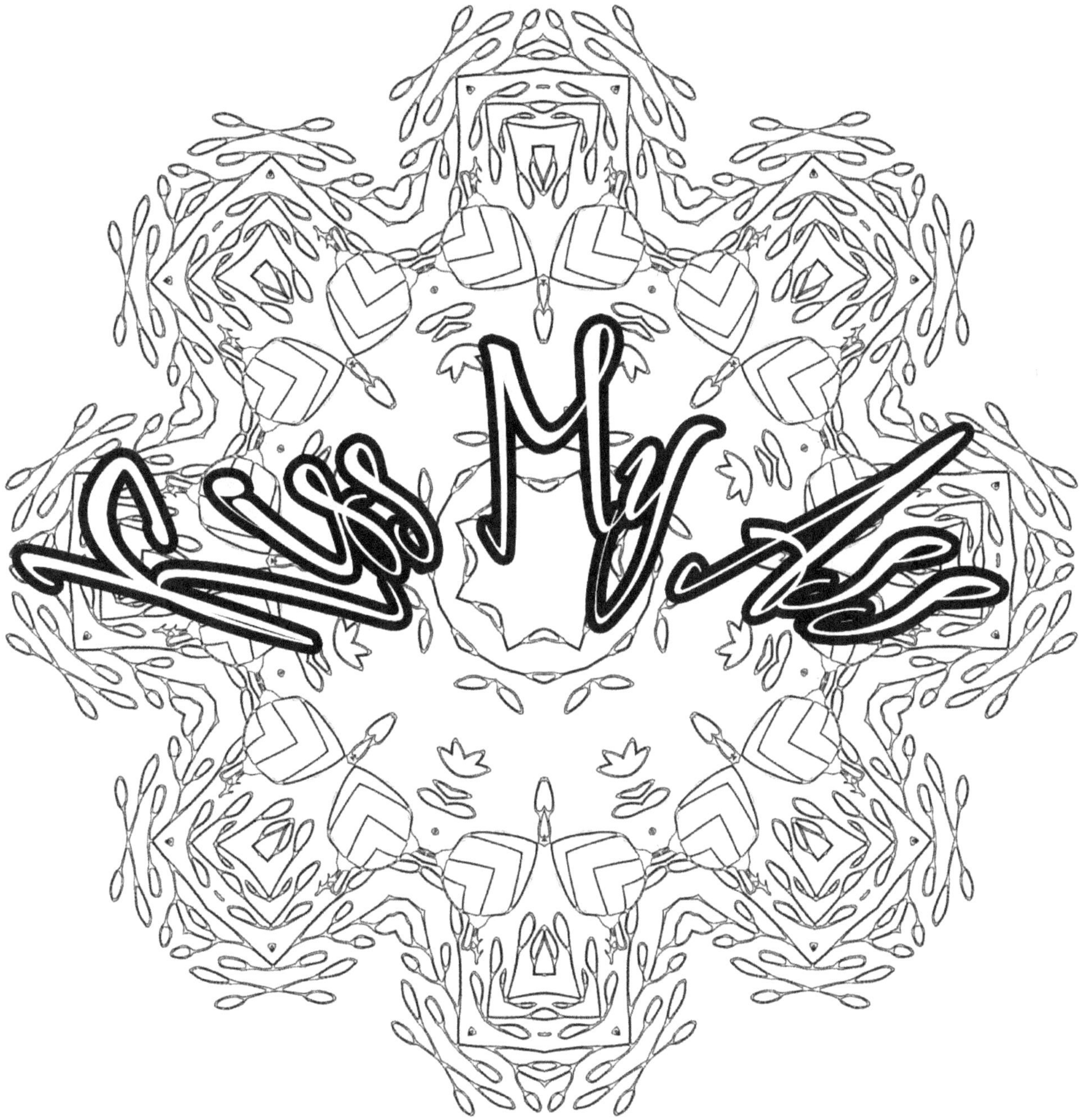
Kiss My Ass

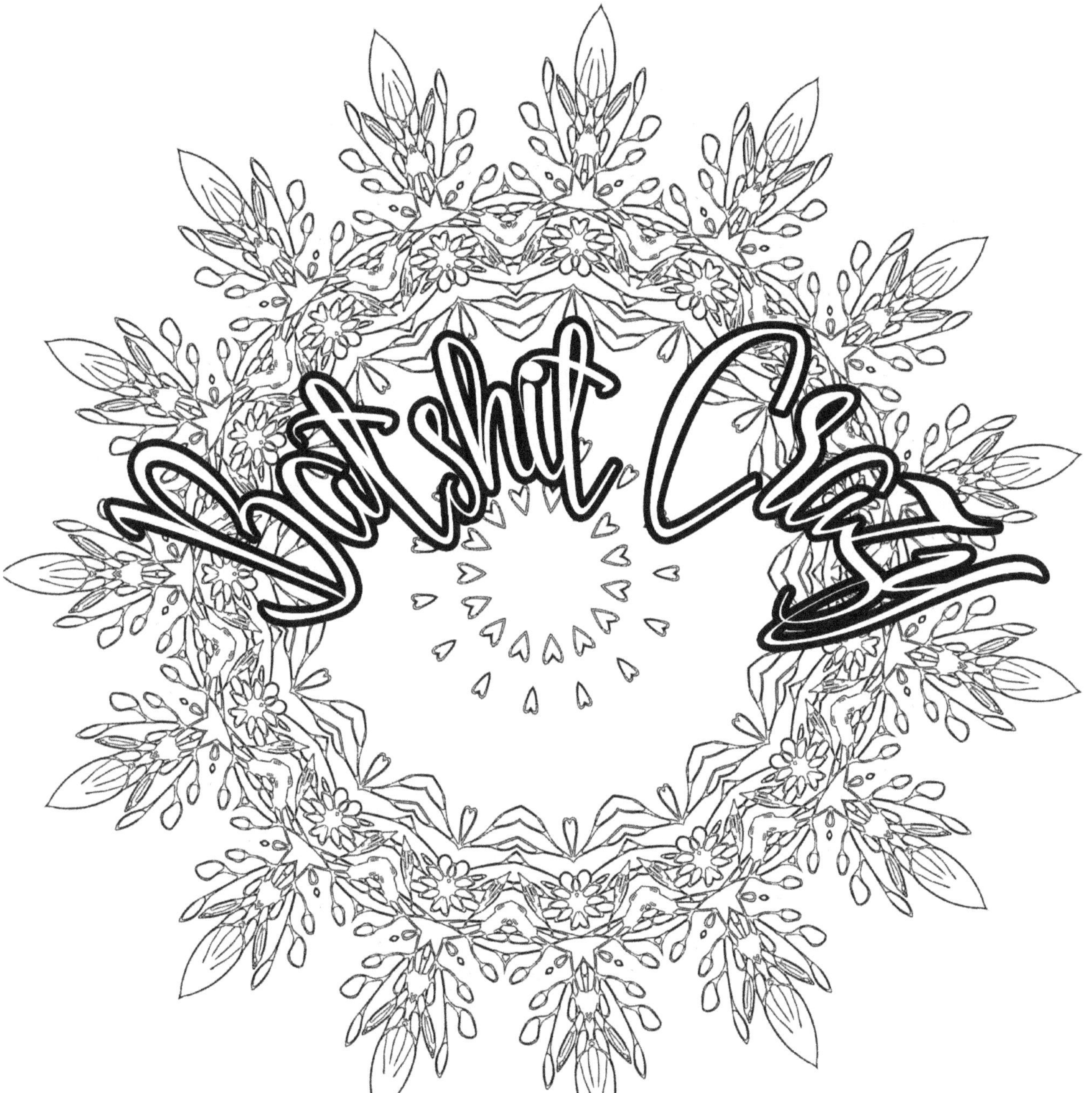
Batshit Crazy

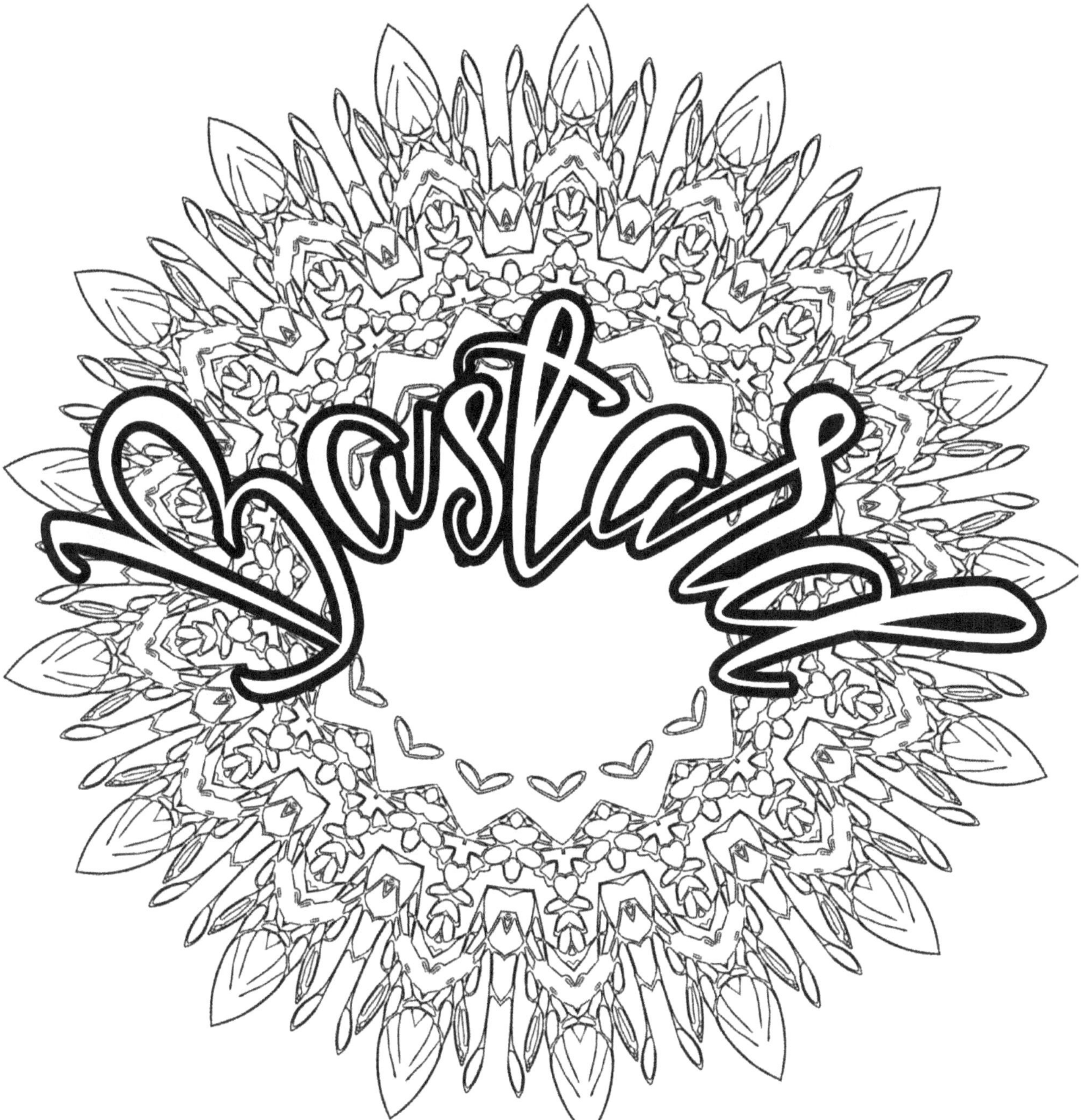
Bastard

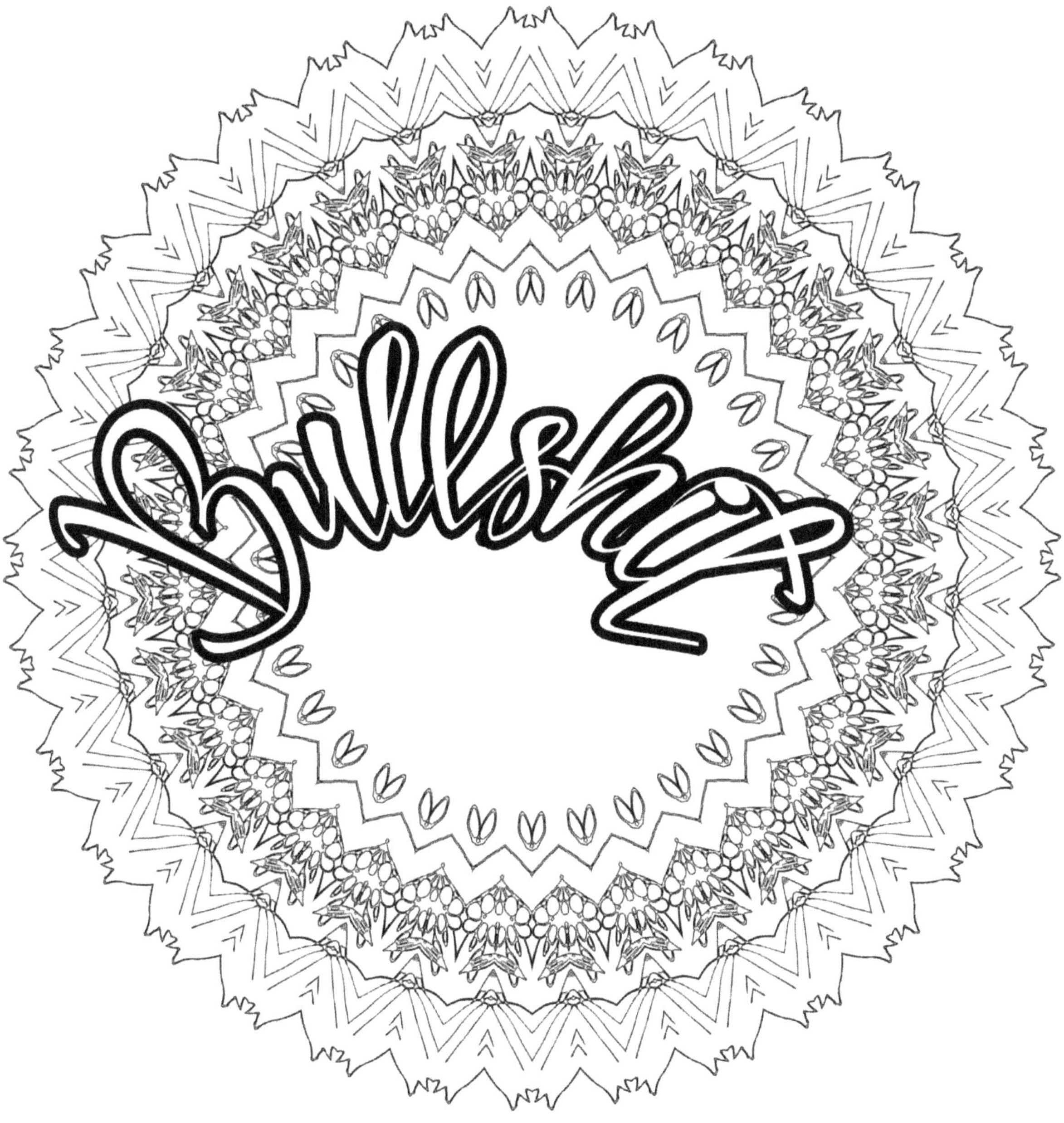
Bullshit

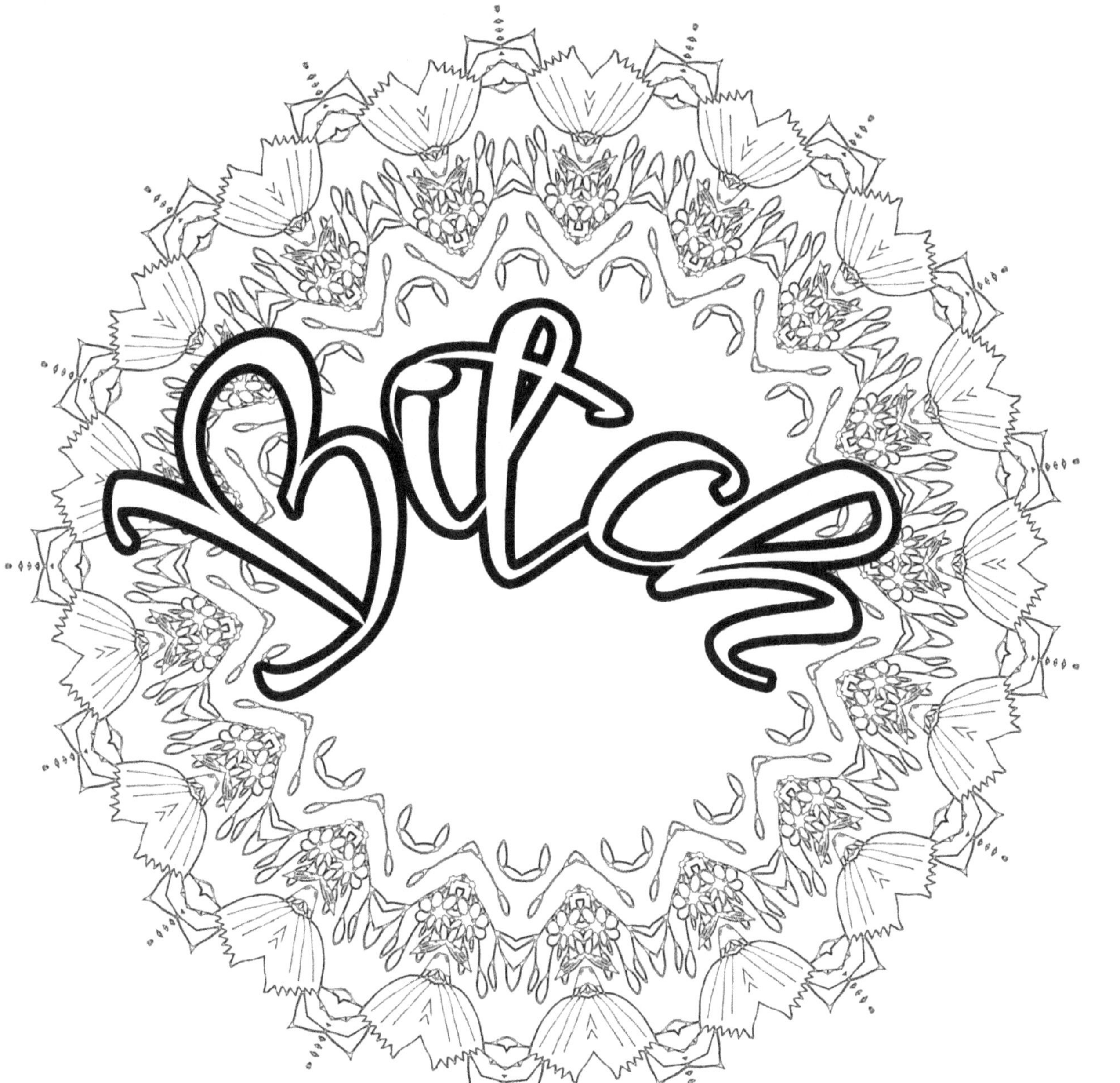
Bitch

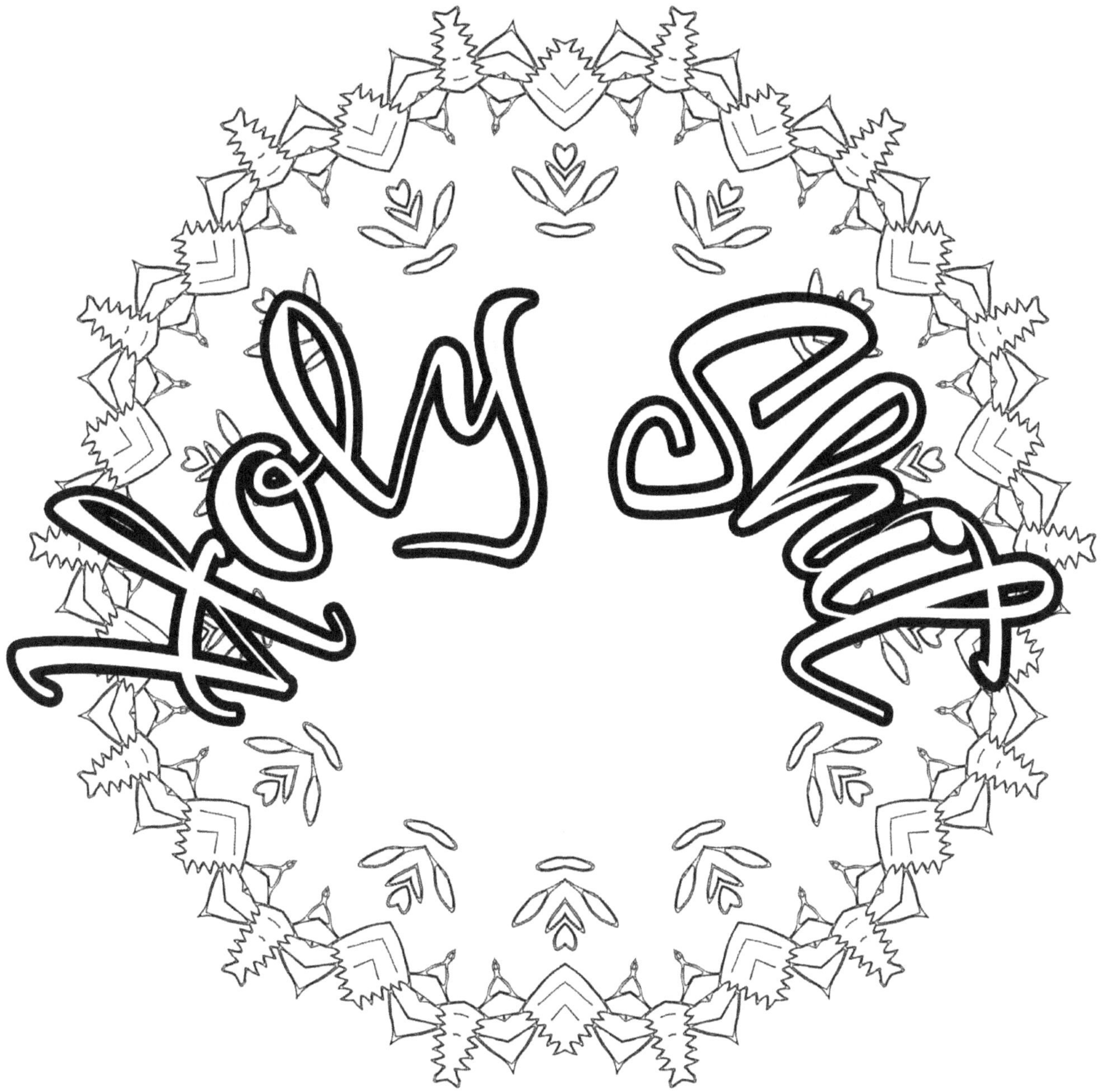
Holy Shit

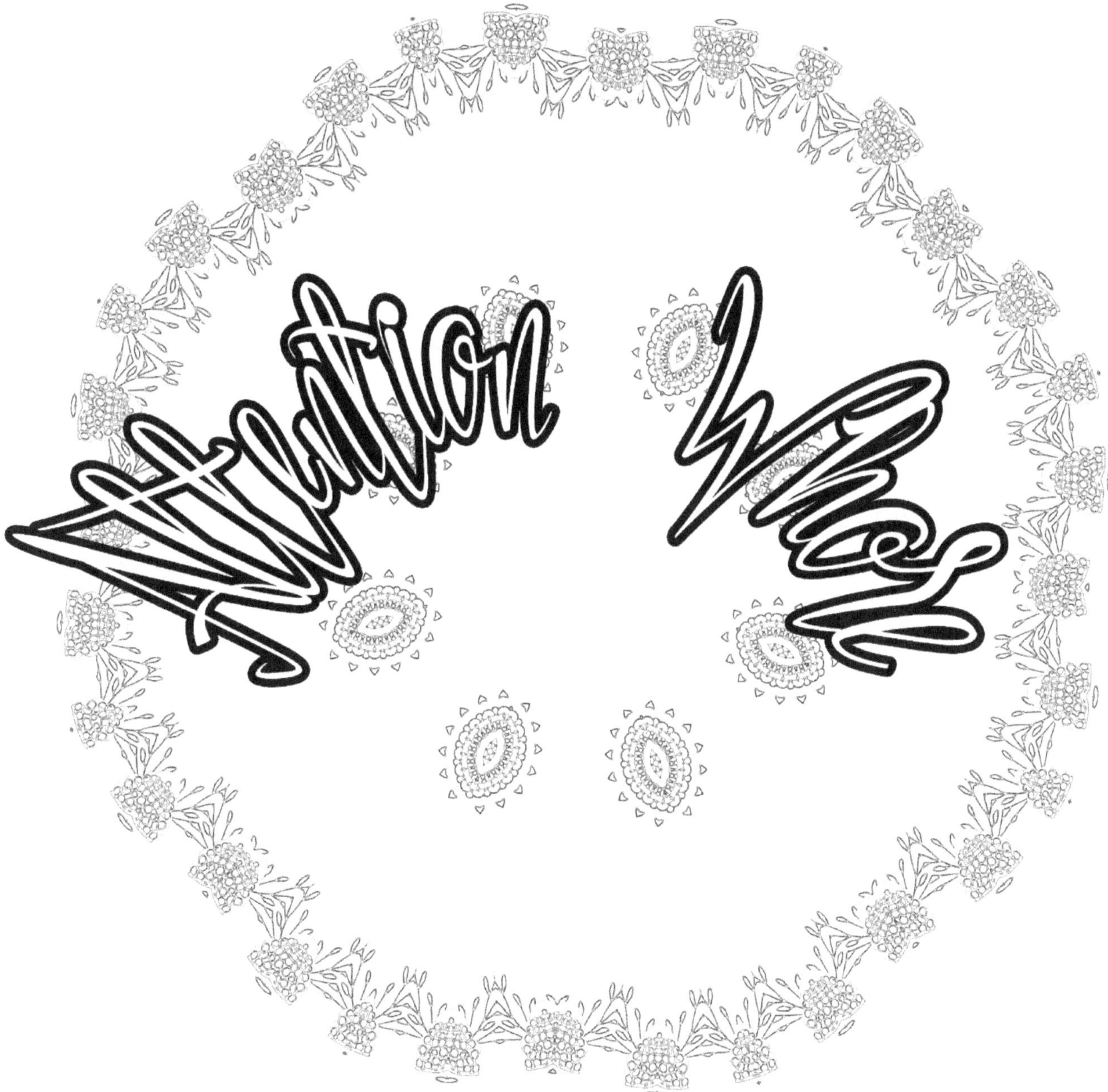

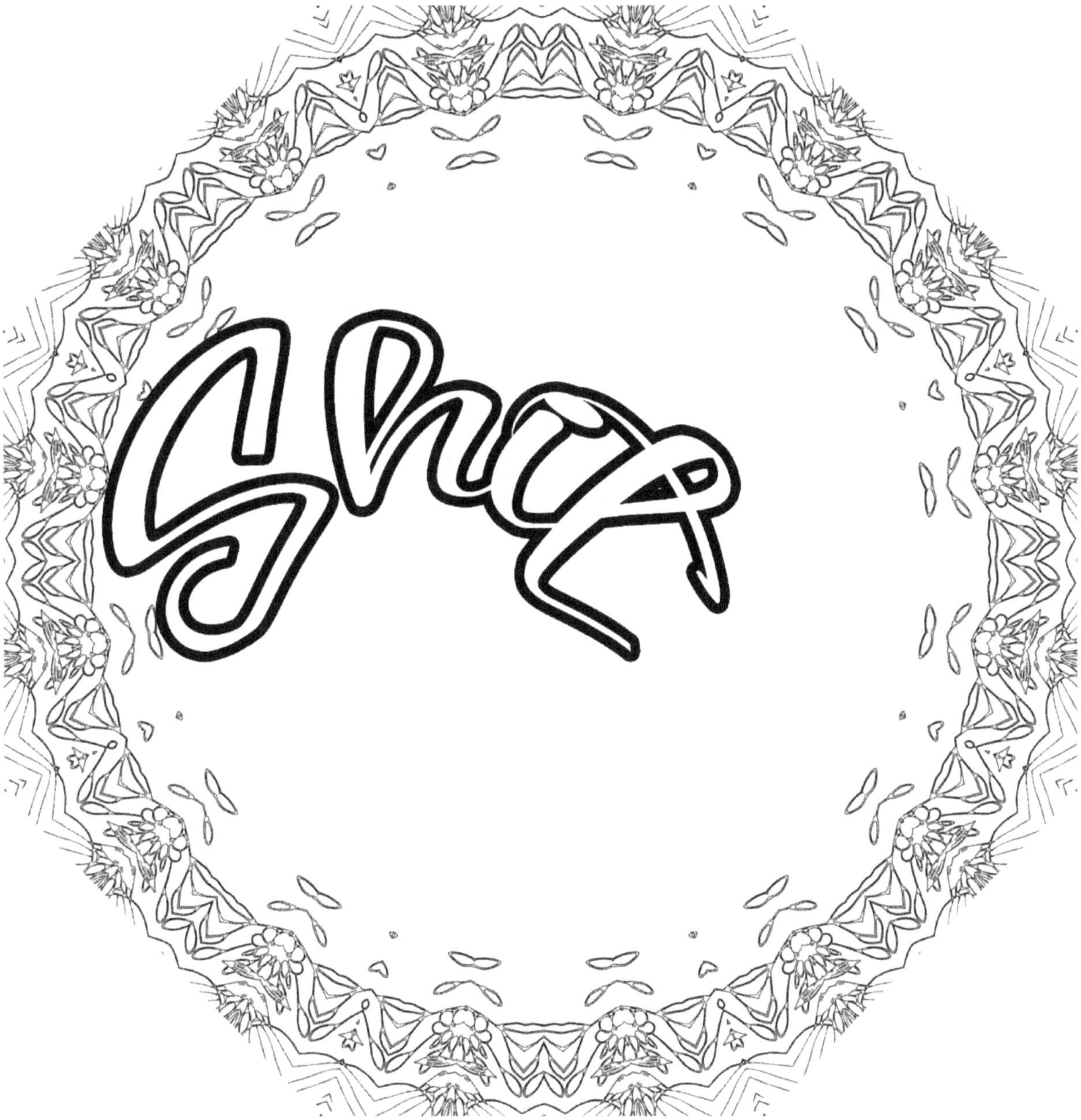
Shit

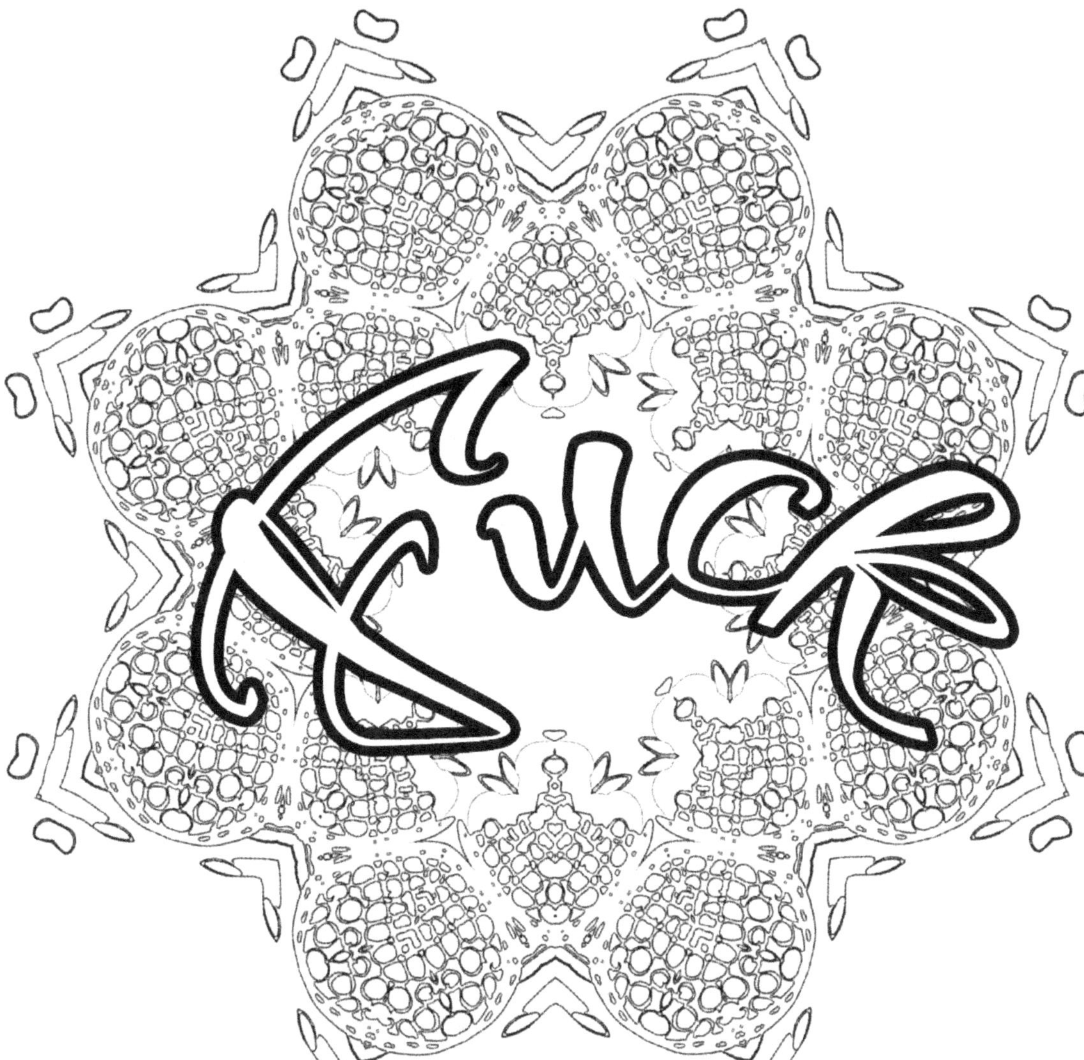
Fuck

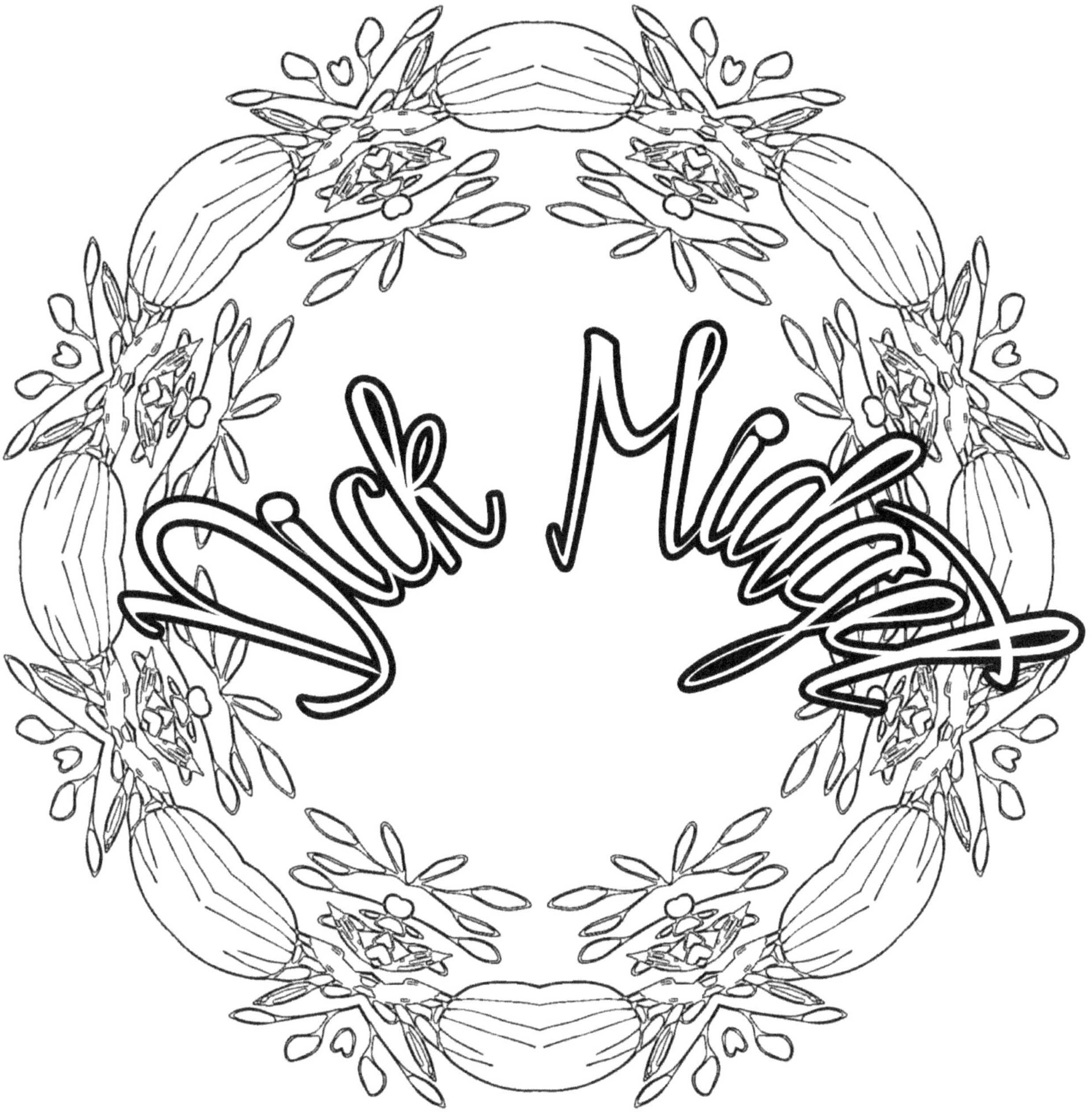
Dick Midget

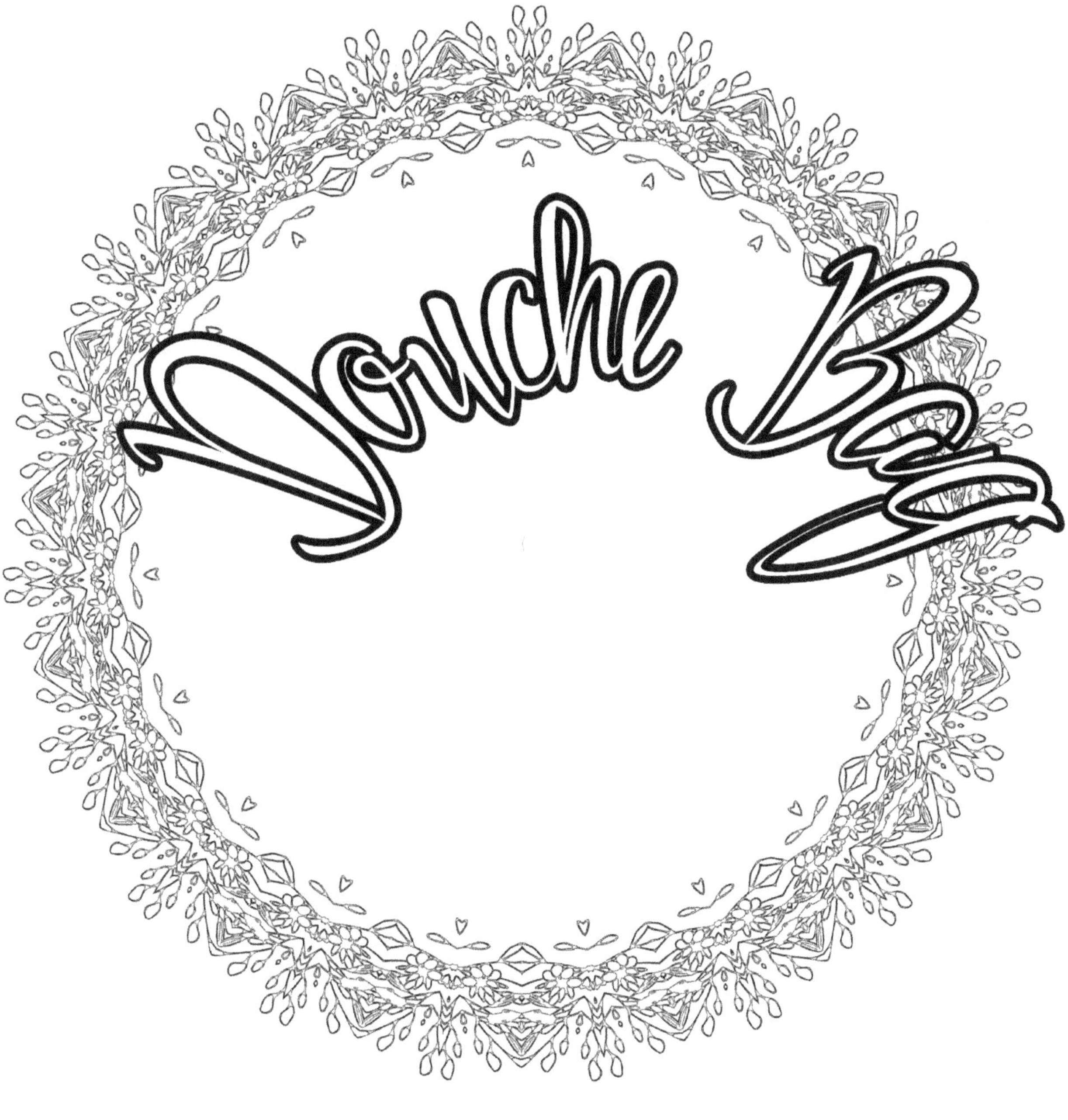
Douche Bag

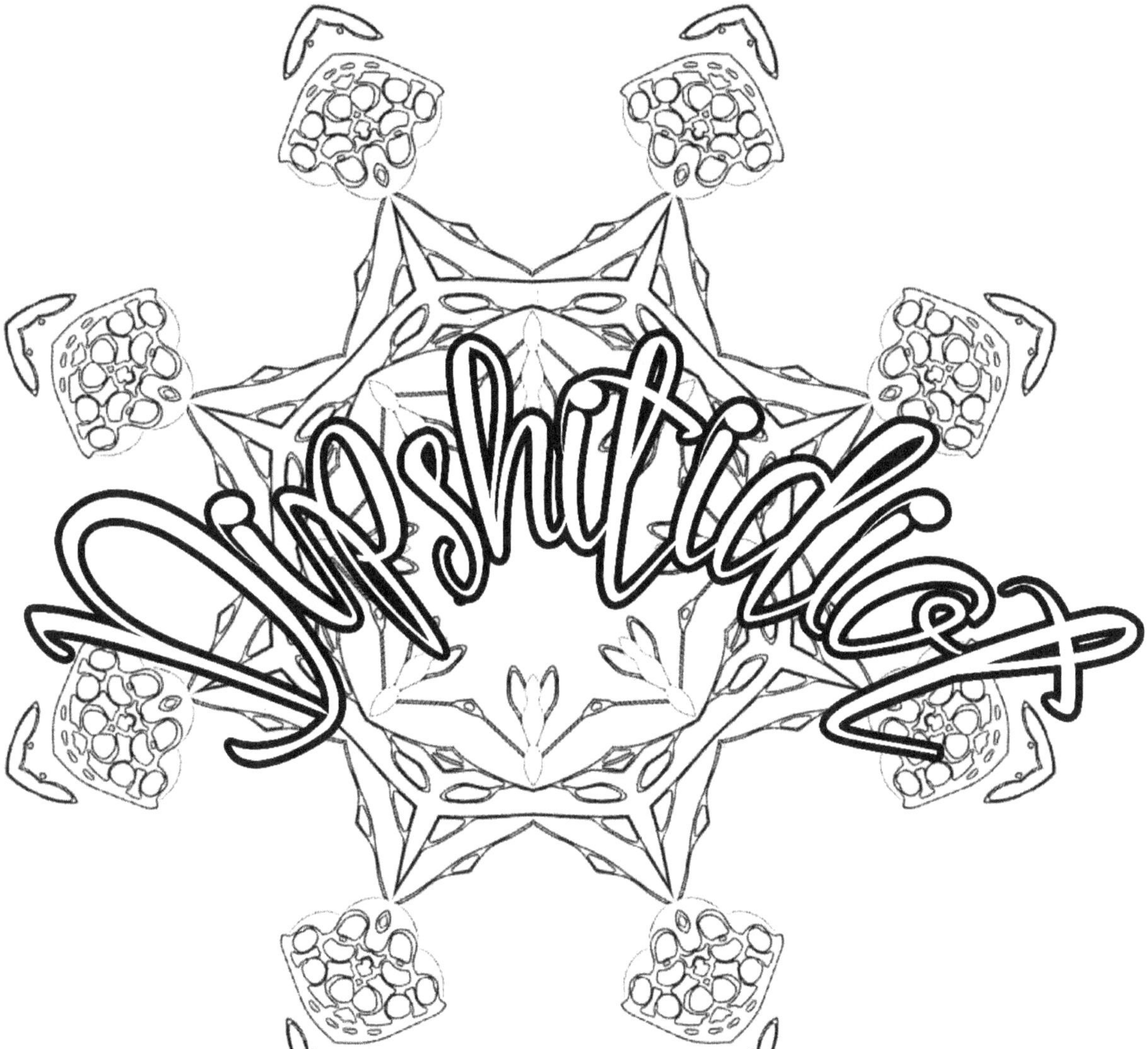
Dipshitidiot

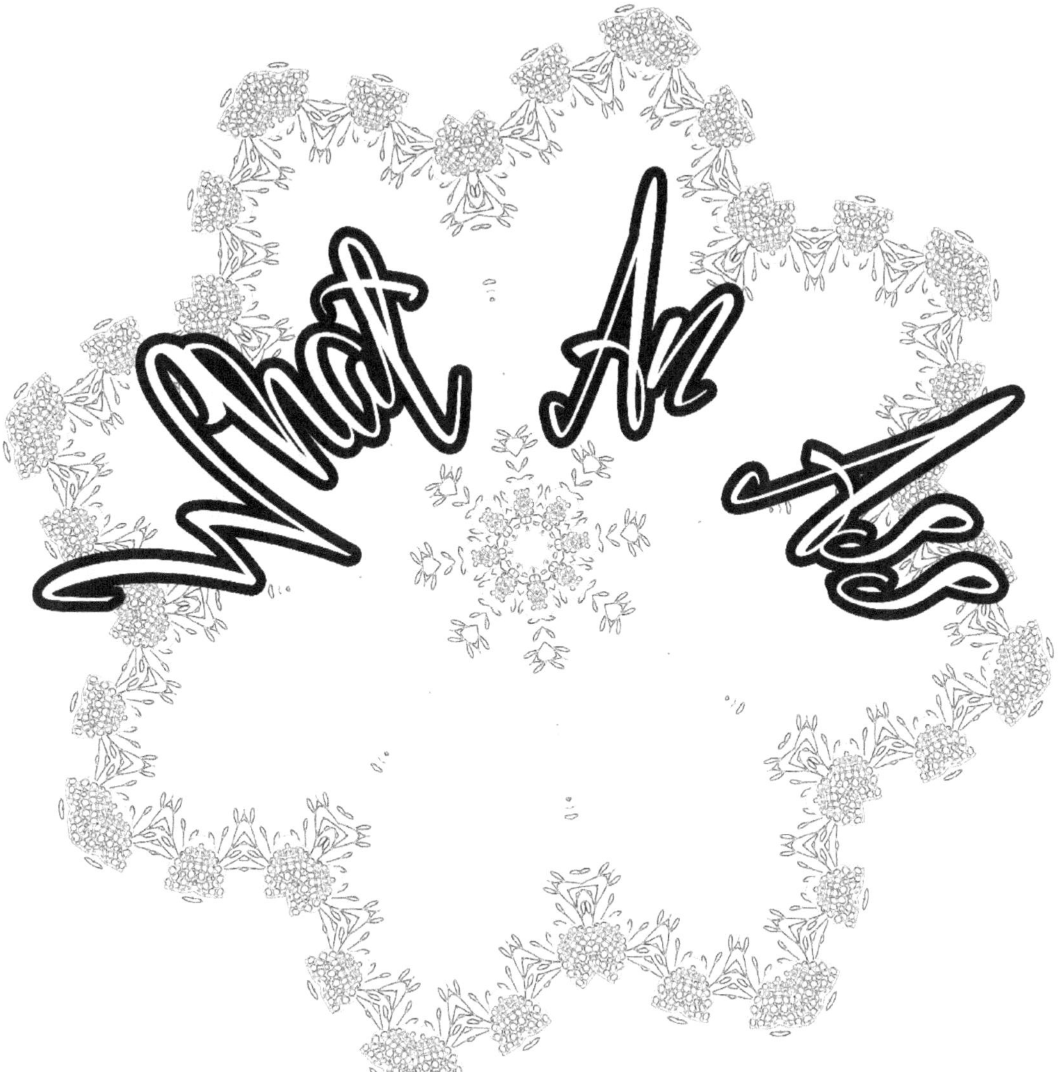
What An Ass

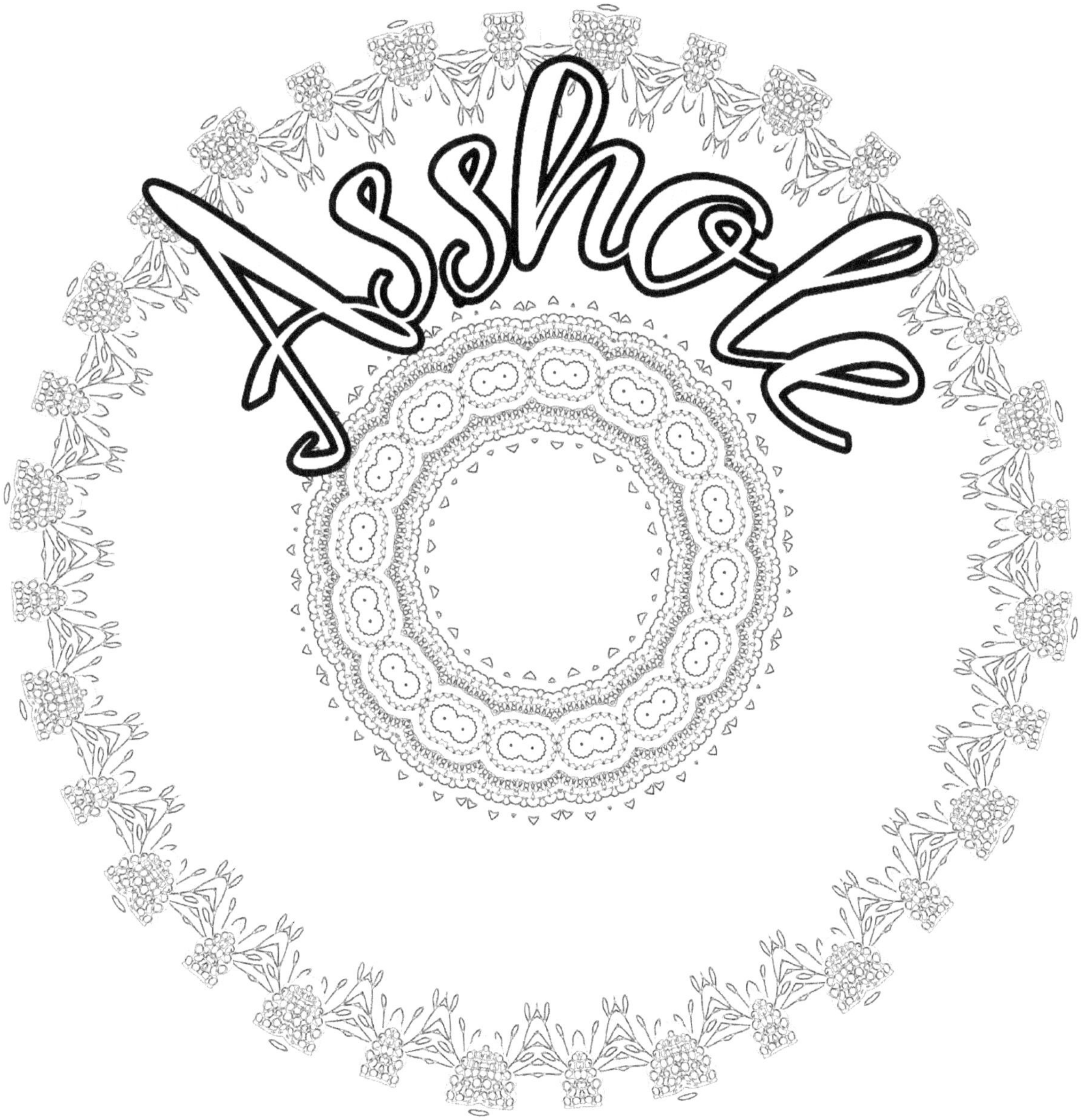
Asshole

www.ingramcontent.com/pod-product-compliance
Lightning Source LLC
Chambersburg PA
CBHW081747170526
45167CB00009B/3951
* 9 7 8 1 5 4 4 1 1 6 2 3 5 *